STUDENT GUIDE

THE LANGUAGE ALGEBRA

EQUATIONS,
TABLES,
AND GRAPHS

$x^2 = y$

MathScape
SEEING AND THINKING
MATHEMATICALLY

D1278439

THE LANGUAGE of ALGEBRA

How can math help you describe and display relationships?

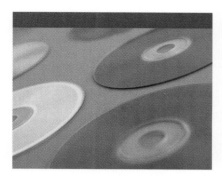

PHASE**ONE**
Writing Equations and Inequalities

In this phase, you will use variables to write equations and inequalities that describe your ideal school. You will also create a list of rules for deciding when two expressions are equivalent. Then you will have a chance to use these tools as you analyze data about the top-selling albums of all time.

PHASE**TWO**
Creating Graphs of Equations

Here you will explore the coordinate plane as another way of describing things. You will move around a coordinate plane following directions given by your teacher. You will use graphing to help explore the relationship between Fahrenheit and Celsius. Finally, you will make a graph showing the future sales of an album.

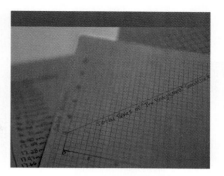

PHASE**THREE**
Finding Solutions of Equations

What does it mean for a number to be a solution of an equation? First, you will explore the idea of a solution in a real-world situation. Then you will develop your own methods for solving equations. At the end of this phase, you will have a chance to use everything you have learned as you predict the future sales of an album.

The 10 Top-Selling Albums of All Time

1. Thriller, Michael Jackson
2. Their Greatest Hits, Eagles
3. Rumours, Fleetwood Mac
4. Led Zeppelin IV, Led Zeppelin
5. The Bodyguard, Soundtrack, Whitney Houston et al.
6. Born in the USA, Bruce Springsteen
7. Boston, Boston
8. Hotel California, Eagles
9. Greatest Hits, Elton John
10. Cracked Rear View, Hootie and the Blowfish

Source: Entertainment Weekly; SoundScan

PHASE ONE

In this phase, you will use variables to write equations and inequalities. These tools will help you describe your ideal school. They will also be useful when you analyze data about the top-selling albums of all time.

Equation writing is an important ingredient in the language of algebra. Scientists often write equations to describe their work. What famous scientific equations can you think of?

Writing Equations and Inequalities

WHAT'S THE MATH?

Investigations in this section focus on:

ALGEBRA

- Using variables to write expressions, equations, and inequalities

- Graphing inequalities on a number line

- Making a table of values that satisfy an equation

- Deciding if two expressions are equivalent

DATA and STATISTICS

- Making a table of data

- Writing an equation to describe data

- Using an equation to make a prediction

1 Describing the Ideal School

How can mathematics be used to help describe the ideal school? You will start by setting up some variables and using them to write expressions. Then you can write equations to describe relationships about the school.

Write Expressions About a School

How can you use variables to write expressions?

You can put variables together with numbers and operations ($+$, $-$, $\times$, and $\div$) to write **expressions.** For example, the expression $b + g$ represents the number of boys plus the number of girls, or the total number of students.

1 Tell what each of the following expressions represents.

a. $t + b + g$

b. pl

c. $(b + g) \div t$

2 Use variables to write an expression for each of the following.

a. the total number of class periods per week

b. the number of teachers who do not teach math

c. the percentage of teachers who teach math

3 Write at least three new expressions that describe a school. You can use the variables listed above, the variables your class added, or completely new variables. If you use new variables, be sure to write down what they represent. Be prepared to share your expressions with the class.

Variables

A **variable** is a letter or symbol that represents a quantity. Here is some information about any school that can be represented by variables.

t = number of teachers at the school

m = number of math teachers at the school

b = number of boys at the school

g = number of girls at the school

p = number of class periods in one day

l = length of one class period, in minutes

Write Equations About the Ideal School

Imagine the school of your dreams. Work with a partner to describe the school using equations.

What equations can you write to help describe the ideal school?

1 Use the variables on page 6 or the variables your class added to write at least five equations that describe your ideal school. On a separate sheet of paper, make an answer key telling what the equations represent.

2 Trade your set of equations with another pair of students. (Hang onto the answer key!) For each of the equations you receive, write a translation of the equation into words.

3 For each equation, make a table showing some sample values that fit the equation.

4 Trade back papers and see if your equations were interpreted correctly. Is there anything you would do differently? Be prepared to discuss this with the class.

1. $g = 2b$
2.
3.
4.
5.

Answer Key
1. There are twice as many girls as boys.
2.
3.
4.
5.

1. $m = 0.35t$
   35% of all teachers are math teachers.
2.

1. $m = 0.35t$
   35% of all teachers are math teachers.

t (teachers)	m (math teachers)
100	35
60	21

Equations

An **equation** describes a relationship between two expressions. An equation tells you that two expressions are equal. Here are some examples.

$g = b + 43$ The number of girls equals the number of boys plus 43.

OR

There are 43 more girls than boys.

$m = \frac{1}{5}t$ The number of math teachers equals one-fifth of the total number of teachers.

OR

One-fifth of all teachers are math teachers.

expression
equation

omework

page 34

2 Not All Things Are Equal

WRITING AND INTERPRETING INEQUALITIES

Equations are useful when you need to relate two expressions that are equal. When two expressions are not equal, the statements you can write are called inequalities. How can the language of inequalities help you say some more about your ideal school?

Express Inequalities in Different Ways

How many ways can you express the same inequality?

Inequalities can be translated into words and can be pictured on a number line. For each of the following, think of as many different ways of saying the same thing as you can. Use words, symbols, and pictures and keep a written record of your results.

1 $x < -2$

2 x is no greater than 4

3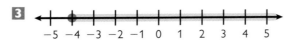

Inequalities

You can use inequalities to compare expressions that are not equal.

Symbol	Example	Number-Line Graph
$<$ less than	$x < 3$ x is less than 3.	$-5\ -4\ -3\ -2\ -1\ \ 0\ \ 1\ \ 2\ \ 3\ \ 4\ \ 5$
$\leq$ less than or equal to	$x \leq 3$ x is less than or equal to 3.	$-5\ -4\ -3\ -2\ -1\ \ 0\ \ 1\ \ 2\ \ 3\ \ 4\ \ 5$
$>$ greater than	$x > 3$ x is greater than 3.	$-5\ -4\ -3\ -2\ -1\ \ 0\ \ 1\ \ 2\ \ 3\ \ 4\ \ 5$
$\geq$ greater than or equal to	$x \geq 3$ x is greater than or equal to 3.	$-5\ -4\ -3\ -2\ -1\ \ 0\ \ 1\ \ 2\ \ 3\ \ 4\ \ 5$

Write Inequalities About the Ideal School

Imagine the school of your dreams. Work with a partner to describe the school using inequalities.

How can you use inequalities to describe the ideal school?

1 Use the variables on page 6 or the variables your class added to the list to write at least five inequalities that describe the ideal school. On a separate sheet of paper (the answer key), keep a record of what the inequalities represent.

1. $b + g \leq 1{,}500$
2.
3.
4.
5.

Answer Key
1. The number of students is less than or equal to 1,500.
2.
3.
4.
5.

2 Write at least five verbal descriptions of inequalities about the school. Then on the answer key, write these inequalities using symbols.

1. $b + g \leq 1{,}500$
2.
3.
4.
5. _____
6. There are at least 10 more girls than boys.
7.

Answer Key
1. The number of students is less than or equal to 1,500.
2.
3.
4.
5. _____
6. $b + 10 \leq g$
7.

3 Trade your set of inequalities and verbal descriptions with another pair of students. (Hang onto the answer key!) For each of the inequalities you receive, write a translation of the inequality into words. For each of the verbal descriptions you receive, write an inequality using symbols.

4 Trade back papers with the other pair of students and see if they interpreted your inequalities and descriptions correctly. Is there anything you would do differently? Be prepared to discuss this with the class.

hot **words** | inequality

Homework

page 35

3 Different Ways to Say the Same Thing

Can two equations look different but say the same thing?
You will have a chance to write some equations that describe simple situations and see how your equations compare to those of your classmates. This will help you create a master list of rules for deciding when two expressions are equivalent.

Write Equations from Situations

Can you write more than one equation to describe a situation?

Write an equation to describe each situation. Then see if you can write another equation that also works.

1 Movable folding chairs in a school auditorium can be arranged in rows with an aisle down the middle. Here are two examples.

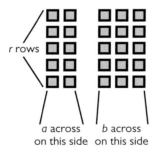

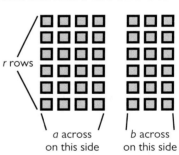

r rows

a across on this side *b* across on this side

r rows

a across on this side *b* across on this side

Write an equation for the total number of chairs, *c*, in the auditorium. Your equation should tell how *c* is related to *r*, *a*, and *b*.

2 A restaurant serves a buffet along a row of square tables. The row of square tables is surrounded by round tables for diners.

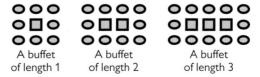

A buffet of length 1   A buffet of length 2   A buffet of length 3

Write an equation that tells how many round tables, *T*, there are for a buffet of length *L*.

Explore Rules for Equivalence

Work with classmates to write a list of rules that can be used to tell whether two expressions are equivalent. Try to state your rules as generally as possible. Begin by considering the following questions. (Remember that two equivalent expressions will give identical results no matter what values are chosen for the variables.)

What rules can you use to decide if two expressions are equivalent?

1. Is $x + y$ equivalent to $y + x$?

2. Is $3(a + b)$ equivalent to $3a + 3b$?

3. Is $m - n$ equivalent to $n - m$?

4. Is $3x + 8x$ equivalent to $11x$?

5. Is $9y - 14y$ equivalent to $-5y$?

6. Is $a - a$ equivalent to 0?

7. Is $\frac{1}{2}x$ equivalent to $\frac{x}{2}$?

8. Is ab equivalent to ba?

9. Is $5 - x$ equivalent to $x - 5$?

10. Is $7(a - b)$ equivalent to $7a - 7b$?

Summarize the Rules

Write your own summary of the rules your class developed for deciding when expressions are equivalent. Include the following:

- a statement of each rule in words

- a statement of each rule using variables

- a specific example of each rule, or anything else that will help you remember how to use it

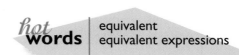

hot **words** | equivalent
equivalent expressions

page 36

4

The Top-Selling Albums of All Time, Part 1

WRITING EQUATIONS TO ANALYZE DATA

How many copies of Elton John's *Greatest Hits* will have been sold by the year 2050? An equation can help answer this question.

Convert the Data to Consistent Units

How can the "Current Rate" data be converted to millions-per-year?

It is useful to have the "Current Rate" data in millions-per-year. These questions will help you convert the data for *Thriller:*

1 If *Thriller* sells 1,800 copies in one week, how many are sold in one year?

2 Is the result greater than or less than 1 million copies?

3 How can you write this amount as a number of millions? Round your answer to the nearest hundredth.

Repeat the process for the other albums. Record your results in a chart.

Top-Selling Albums of All Time in the U.S.

Rank	Album, Artist	Year Released	Total Sold Through 1996	Current Rate of Sale
1	*Thriller*, Michael Jackson	1982	24 million	1,800 per week
2	*Their Greatest Hits*, Eagles	1976	22 million	4,400 per week
3	*Rumours*, Fleetwood Mac	1977	17 million	2,500 per week
4	*Led Zeppelin IV*, Led Zeppelin	1971	16 million	3,800 per week
5	*The Bodyguard* Soundtrack, Whitney Houston et al.	1992	15 million	3,600 per week
6	*Born in the USA*, Bruce Springsteen	1984	15 million	1,100 per week
7	*Boston*, Boston	1976	15 million	2,300 per week
8	*Hotel California*, Eagles	1976	14 million	4,200 per week
9	*Greatest Hits*, Elton John	1974	13 million	4,000 per week
10	*Cracked Rear View*, Hootie and the Blowfish	1994	13 million	45,000 per week

Source: *Entertainment Weekly Magazine; SoundScan*

Write an Equation to Predict Sales

Choose one album that you would like to work with. Then follow these steps to write an equation that describes the album's sales.

What equation can you write to help predict the sales of an album?

1 Make a table that shows the total sales for your album 0 years, 1 year, 2 years, 3 years, 4 years, 5 years, and 10 years after 1996.

Sales for Hotel California	
Years Beyond 1996	Total Sales (millions)
0 (1996)	14
1 (1997)	14.22
2 (1998)	14.44
3 (1999)	14.66
4 (2000)	14.88
5 (2001)	15.1
...	
10 (2006)	

2 How could you find the total sales for your album for any given number of years after 1996?

3 Write an equation that relates x, the number of years after 1996, to y, the total sales for that year.

4 Use your equation to predict the total sales of your album in the year 2050.

Be sure to save your work. You will need it later in this unit!

Write About the Results

Write one or two paragraphs that summarize the thinking you used in this lesson. Include answers to these questions:

- How did you find the equation describing your album's total sales?

- How did you use this equation to predict your album's sales in the year 2050?

- How realistic do you think your prediction is? Do you think the actual total sales in 2050 will be greater than or less than the amount you predicted? Why?

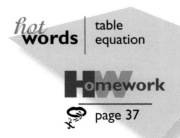

hot **words** | table equation

Homework

🌀 page 37

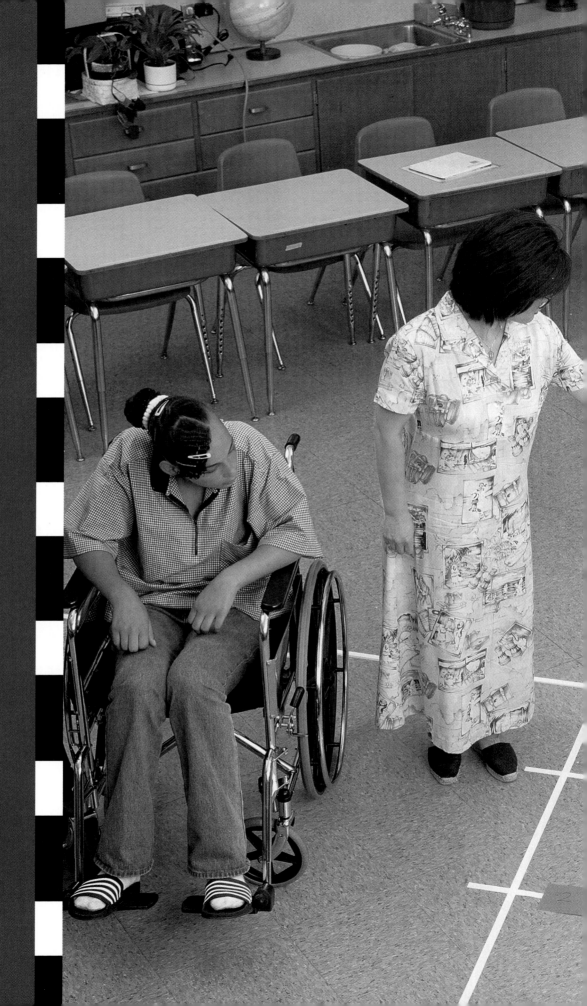

PHASE TWO

In this phase, you will explore the coordinate plane. You will see how the coordinate plane is connected to words, tables, and equations. By the end of the phase, you will be able to make a graph that shows the future sales of an album.

The coordinate plane is a grid that helps you describe the location of objects. What are some ways grids are used to describe locations in everyday life?

Creating Graphs of Equations

WHAT'S THE MATH?

Investigations in this section focus on:

ALGEBRA

- Plotting and naming points on the coordinate plane

- Making a graph of an equation

- Graphing horizontal and vertical lines

- Working back and forth among words, tables, equations, and graphs

DATA and STATISTICS

- Making a coordinate graph to display and analyze data

- Using a graph to make a prediction

5 Seeing Things Graphically

The coordinate plane is another important tool in algebra. Just like variables, tables, and equations, the coordinate plane gives you a way to describe and analyze situations. First you will explore the basics of the coordinate plane. Then you will see what happens when you plot points that fit an equation.

Explore Facts About the Coordinate Plane

What facts can you write about points on the coordinate plane?

What can you say about the coordinates of points that lie . . .

1 in the second quadrant?

2 on the *x*-axis?

3 on the *y*-axis?

4 to the left of the *y*-axis?

For each of the above questions, plot some points on the coordinate plane that fit the description. Write the coordinates of these points and ask yourself what the coordinates have in common. Write a short statement about each of your findings.

The Coordinate Plane

The **coordinate plane** is divided into four **quadrants** by the horizontal **x-axis** and the vertical **y-axis**. The axes intersect at the **origin**. You can locate any **point** on the plane if you know the **coordinates** for *x* and *y*. The *x*-coordinate is always stated first.

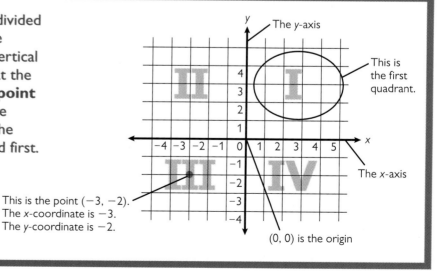

The *y*-axis

This is the first quadrant.

The *x*-axis

This is the point (−3, −2). The *x*-coordinate is −3. The *y*-coordinate is −2.

(0, 0) is the origin

Plot Points from an Equation

Your teacher will give you an equation to work with for this investigation. Follow these steps to make a graph of your equation.

What happens when you plot ordered pairs that come from an equation?

1 Begin by making a table of values that satisfy the equation. You should have at least ten pairs of numbers, including some negative values.

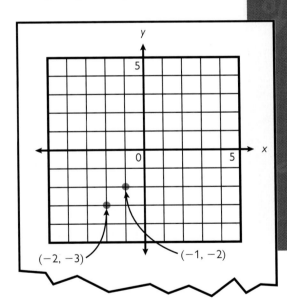

$y = x - 1$

x	y
−2	−3
−1	−2
0	−1
1	

2 Turn your table into a list of ordered pairs.

x	y	
−2	−3	⟶ (−2, −3)
−1	−2	⟶ (−1, −2)
0	−1	
1	0	

3 Plot each of the points on the same coordinate grid.

(−2, −3)   (−1, −2)

4 What do you notice about your points? If you find more ordered pairs that satisfy your equation, do you think the new points will have the same property?

hot **words** | coordinates
ordered pair

Homework
page 38

6 The Algebra Walk

GRAPHING LINEAR EQUATIONS

Now you and your classmates will do a physical experiment to find out more about graphs. As you experiment, be sure to take notes on what you see. Then you will graph some equations by hand and compare results.

Do the Algebra Walk

What do you notice when your classmates move on a coordinate plane as directed by your teacher?

To do this experiment, your teacher will choose nine students to be "walkers." The other students are observers.

If you are a walker . . .

1 Stand at one of the integers on the *x*-axis that is marked on the floor. This is your **starting number.** Be sure to face in the direction of the positive *y*-axis.

2 Your teacher will give you directions on how to get a **walking number.** If your walking number is positive, move directly forward that many units. If your walking number is negative, move directly backward that many units. If your walking number is zero, stay put!

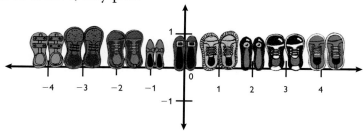

If you are an observer . . .

1 Watch carefully as your classmates move to their new positions on the coordinate plane.

2 Record their final positions with dots on your Algebra Walk Recording Sheet.

Graph Some Equations

For each of the following equations, make a table of values that fit the equation. Then make a graph of the equation.

1. $y = 2x$

2. $y = -2x$

3. $y = 2x + 1$

4. $y = 2x - 1$

5. $y = x + 1$

6. $y = -x + 1$

Compare the graphs you made to the results you recorded on your Algebra Walk Recording Sheet. Write a few sentences about what you notice.

How do the graphs of some equations compare to the results of the Algebra Walk?

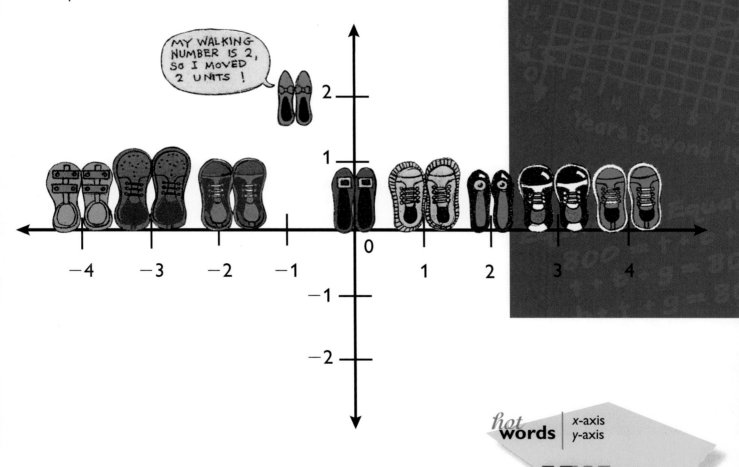

MY WALKING NUMBER IS 2, SO I MOVED 2 UNITS!

hot **words** | x-axis
y-axis

Homework
page 39

7 Putting It All Together

How are words, tables, equations, and graphs connected?

First you will use these tools to explore horizontal and vertical lines. Then you will work with all four tools to explore the relationship between Fahrenheit and Celsius.

Explore Horizontal and Vertical Lines

What do the equations of horizontal and vertical lines look like?

What do equations, tables, and graphs look like when the lines they represent are horizontal or vertical? Work on the following items with a partner to help answer this question.

1 Make a table of values for the equation $y = 4$. Then create a graph for the equation.

2 Find the coordinates of at least five points on the line shown below. Use these coordinates to set up a table of x and y values. Look at your table. What do you notice? What equation do you think corresponds to this line?

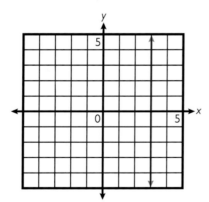

Show a Relationship in Four Different Ways

The equation $F = \frac{9}{5}C + 32$ describes the relationship between Fahrenheit and Celsius.

1 Write a description of the relationship between Fahrenheit and Celsius in words.

2 Make a table showing at least five pairs of values for Celsius (C) and Fahrenheit (F).

3 Make a graph that shows the relationship between Fahrenheit and Celsius. You will need to choose an appropriate scale for the axes on your graph.

A temperature of 0° Celsius is the same as a temperature of 32° Fahrenheit. How is this shown in each of your representations? Be ready to discuss this with the class.

How can words, tables, equations, and graphs help describe the relationship between Fahrenheit and Celsius?

Fahrenheit and Celsius

Temperatures are usually measured in degrees Fahrenheit or degrees Celsius.

Celsius   Fahrenheit

Water boils at 100° Celsius, which is the same as 212° Fahrenheit. — 100   212

Water freezes at 0° Celsius, which is the same as 32° Fahrenheit. — 0   32

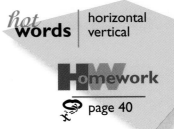

hot **words**   horizontal
vertical

Homework

page 40

8 The Top-Selling Albums of All Time, Part 2

MAKING GRAPHS TO ANALYZE DATA

How can you use a graph to display and analyze data?

You will use tables and equations to make a graph that helps you analyze the sales of an album. Then you will summarize what you know about words, tables, equations, and graphs—the four main tools of algebra.

Make a Graph of Future Sales

What does the graph of an album's future sales look like?

You have already made a table and written an equation that describe the sales of an album. Now use this information to make a graph.

1 Choose a scale for the *x*-axis and *y*-axis. The *x*-axis should show the number of years beyond 1996. (Be sure your graph goes out to at least the year 2010.) The *y*-axis should show total sales.

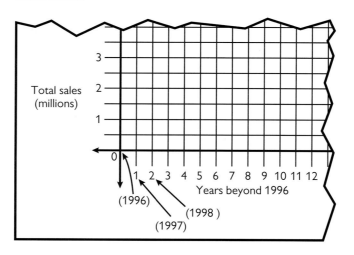

2 Plot some points based on your table of future sales data.

3 Complete the graph of your album's future sales.

According to your graph, approximately how many copies of the album will have been sold in the year 2010?

Write About the Four Representations

You have seen four different ways to describe a situation: words, tables, equations, and graphs. These are called *representations*.

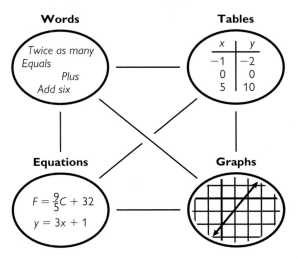

Write a summary of your work with the four representations. Include the following ideas:

- a specific example of when you used each representation

- advantages and disadvantages of each representation

- a description of how to go from an equation to a table to a graph

hot **words** | predict
coordinate graph

Homework
page 41

PHASE THREE

In this phase, you will explore the idea of a solution. You will develop your own methods for solving equations and see how to use the solution of an equation.

Finding the solution of an equation is one of the most useful tools in algebra. At the end of this phase, you will revisit the top-selling albums of all time. You will be able to write and solve an equation to help you predict when an album will reach sales of 30 million copies.

Finding Solutions of Equations

WHAT'S THE MATH?

Investigations in this section focus on:

ALGEBRA

- Understanding what a solution is

- Checking the solution of an equation

- Finding solutions of equations using various methods

- Finding and graphing solutions of inequalities

- Applying solutions in real-world situations

DATA and STATISTICS

- Solving an equation to make a prediction about data

9 Situations and Solutions

How can the tools you have been exploring be used to solve problems? First you will solve a problem about rollerblade rentals. Then you will look more closely at what a solution is and use your own methods to find solutions.

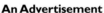

Solve a Rollerblade Rental Problem

How can you use tables, equations, and graphs to solve a problem?

Refer to the advertisement for RolloRentals.

1 Make a table of values that shows the number of hours (*h*) and the corresponding cost (*c*) of a rollerblade rental.

2 Write an equation that describes the relationship between *h* and *c*.

3 Make a graph that shows the relationship between *h* and *c*.

Suppose you have $21 to spend. How long can you rent rollerblades from RolloRentals? Use your table, equation, or graph—or any other method you like— to help solve this problem.

An Advertisement

Solve Some More Rental Problems

For each amount of money, how many hours can you rent rollerblades from RolloRentals? (Note that RolloRentals will rent rollerblades for parts of an hour.)

1. $16

2. $28.50

3. $24.75

4. $106

How did you solve these problems? Write a short description of your method and be ready to discuss it with the class.

Another Advertisement

How can you find the number of rental hours for different amounts of money?

hot **words** | solution

Home**w**ork
page 42

10 Solving Simple Equations and Inequalities

You have seen how to find a solution by making a table or graph. However, it is often useful to find a solution directly from an equation. You will explore some simple equations and develop your own methods for solving them. Then you will do the same for inequalities.

Find Solutions of Simple Equations

What methods can you use to solve simple equations?

Work with classmates to find a value of x that solves each equation. Use any methods that make sense to you, but be ready to share your thinking with the class. Be sure to check your solutions.

1. $6 + 2x = 20$
2. $42 = 10 + 4x$
3. $24 = 1.5x + 6$
4. $-4 + 3x = 11$
5. $3x = -18$
6. $-2x + 5 = 15$

Solutions of Equations

A **solution** of an equation is a value of the variable that makes the equation true.

For example, $x = 4$ is a solution to the equation $3x + 7 = 19$ because $3 \cdot 4 + 7 = 19$.

Write About Equation-Solution Methods

What method or methods can you use to solve equations like the ones shown above? Write a step-by-step description of the thinking you can use to solve these types of equations.

Find Solutions to Simple Inequalities

Work with classmates to find values of x that make each inequality true. Use any methods that make sense to you, but be ready to share your thinking with the class. Graph your solutions on a number line.

What methods can you use to solve simple inequalities?

1. $2x > 8$

2. $6 \leq 3x$

3. $x + 4 > 5$

4. $x - 1 \leq 7$

5. $x + 3 < 0$

6. $2x + 1 < 9$

Solutions of Inequalities

A **solution** of an inequality is a set of values of the variable that make the inequality true.

For example, for the inequality $5x > 10$, any value of x greater than 2 makes this a true inequality. So, the solution is $x > 2$. This solution is shown on the number line.

$$\begin{array}{ccccccccccc} \leftarrow\!\!\!\!\!\! & | & | & | & | & | & | & \circ & | & | & \!\!\!\!\!\!\rightarrow \\ -5 & -4 & -3 & -2 & -1 & 0 & 1 & 2 & 3 & 4 & 5 \end{array}$$

Write About Inequality-Solution Methods

What method or methods can you use to solve inequalities like the ones shown above? Write a step-by-step description of the thinking you can use to solve these types of inequalities.

hot **words** | solution | inequality

Homework

page 43

11 The Balancing Act

Sometimes you can find the solution of a simple equation just by thinking about it logically. For more complex equations, it is helpful to have a method that you can rely on. You will begin by solving some balance problems. Then you will see how the idea of a balance can help you solve equations.

Perform a Balancing Act

How can you find a quantity that makes each scale balance?

Each picture shows a perfectly balanced scale. The cups contain an unknown number of marbles. In each picture, each cup contains the same number of marbles. Work with classmates to figure out how many marbles a cup contains in each picture.

1

2

3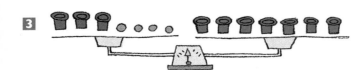

Solve Some Equations

Solve each equation using whatever methods make the most sense to you. You might translate each equation into a balance picture and then find the number of marbles each cup must contain in order to keep the balance. Keep a step-by-step record of your work and check your solutions.

How can you use the idea of a balance to solve equations?

1. $2x + 6 = 3x + 2$

2. $8y + 2 = 2y + 14$

3. $25 = 7 + 3s$

4. $5m + 3 = 3m + 4$

Balance Pictures

Here's how to turn an equation (for example, $2x + 4 = 3x + 3$) into a balance picture.

1. Think of the variable as a cup containing an unknown number of marbles.

x is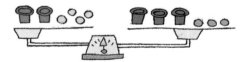

2. Draw each expression as a set of cups and marbles.

$2x + 4$ is  $3x + 3$ is

3. The equation says that the two expressions balance.

hot **words** | equation solution

Homework

page 44

12 The Top-Selling Albums of All Time, Part 3

USING ALGEBRA TO MAKE A PREDICTION

It's time to look at the top-selling albums again. When will the album that you have been working with hit sales of 30 million? To answer this question, you will use everything you know about tables, graphs, equations, and solutions.

Use Tables and Graphs

How can a table and graph help you make a prediction?

When will the album that you have been working with reach total sales of 30 million copies?

1 Make a table showing the future sales of your album. Your table does not need to show every year, but should include the year in which sales hit (or pass) 30 million copies.

2 Make a graph of the future sales of your album. Be sure your graph shows when sales hit 30 million copies.

Based on your table and graph, when do you predict that your album will reach sales of 30 million copies?

Solve an Equation

Now use an equation to help predict when your album will reach sales of 30 million copies.

1 Write an equation that describes the future sales of your album.

2 Modify this equation so that it tells when sales will be 30 million copies.

3 Solve the equation. Keep a record of the steps you used to find the solution.

From your solution of the equation, when do you predict that your album will reach sales of 30 million copies?

How can you solve an equation to help make a prediction?

Write a Report

Imagine that you work for the recording company that makes your album. Write a report of your findings to the company's president. Be sure to include the following:

- your prediction for when sales will reach 30 million copies

- a summary of each method you used to help make this prediction

- a discussion of the strengths and weaknesses of each method

- a discussion of how accurate you think your prediction is

hot **words** | equation
solution

H⊙mework
✎ page 45

Describing the Ideal School

Applying Skills

These variables represent information about a particular math class.

s = number of students in the class.

g = number of girls in the class.

r = number of students in the class with red hair.

b = number of students in the class with black hair.

t = number of textbooks given to each student.

h = number of hours of classes each day.

Tell what each of the following expressions represents.

1. $s - g$ **2.** $b + r$

3. $5h$ **4.** st

5. $s - b$ **6.** $(g \div s) \times 100$

Write an expression for each of the following:

7. the number of students who do not have red hair

8. the number of textbooks handed out to girls

9. the number of minutes of classes each day

10. the number of textbooks handed out to boys

11. the percentage of students who have black hair

Write an equation that says . . .

12. there are 16 more students with black hair than students with red hair.

13. there are twice as many students as girls.

14. 40% of the students have black hair.

Translate each equation into words. Then make a table showing four pairs of sample values that fit the equation.

15. $s = b + 21$ **16.** $b = 4r$ **17.** $s = 2g + 5$

Extending Concepts

18. a. Write an equation that says that y is equal to 25% of x. Then make a table of values that fit the equation. For x, pick whole numbers ranging from 1 to 10. Write y as a decimal.

b. Repeat part **a.** This time, use fractions instead of decimals.

19. Does it make sense for any of the variables listed at the top of the page to take values that are not whole numbers? If so, which ones?

Making Connections

20. The gravity on Jupiter is 2.64 times the gravity on Earth. This can be represented by the equation $J = 2.64E$. Make a table of values that fit the equation. If a person weighs 125 lbs on Earth, how much would the person weigh on Jupiter?

Not All Things Are Equal

Applying Skills

Tell which of the symbols $<$, $>$, or $=$ could go in the blank.

1. 4 __ 9   **2.** 8 __ 3

3. -8 __ -6 **4.** -2 __ 1

5. -0.1 __ -0.2 **6.** 8 __ 8

7. $\frac{2}{3}$ __ $\frac{4}{6}$ **8.** -1 __ 0

An algebraic inequality can be represented by words, symbols, or a number-line graph.

$x < 4$

x is less than 4.

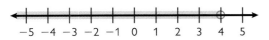

Use words to write each inequality. Express it in as many different ways as you can. Then make a number-line graph.

9. $x > 2$ **10.** $x < 5$

11. $x \leq -1$ **12.** $x \geq -3$

Write each inequality using symbols and make a number-line graph.

13. x is greater than zero.   **14.** x is less than or equal to -3.

15. x is no less than 4.   **16.** x is less than 3.

17. x is no greater than -2.

Use words and symbols to write each inequality.

18.
```
 -5 -4 -3 -2 -1  0  1  2  3  4  5
```

19.
```
 -5 -4 -3 -2 -1  0  1  2  3  4  5
```

Extending Concepts

Suppose that g represents the number of girls in a particular class and b represents the number of boys. Write each inequality in items **20–22** using symbols. Then list all the possibilities for the number of girls if the number of boys is 20.

20. The number of girls is less than or equal to half the number of boys.

21. The number of girls is less than 2 more than the number of boys.

22. The number of boys is at least 3 times the number of girls.

23. Write four inequalities of your own using the variables g and b. Write each one using symbols and using words. Use each operation (addition, subtraction, multiplication, division) at least once.

Making Connections

24. As the moon goes around the earth, the distance between the earth and the moon varies. When the moon is closest to the earth, the distance is 227,000 miles. Use the letter d to write an inequality describing the distance of the moon from the earth.

35

Different Ways to Say the Same Thing

Applying Skills

Tell whether the two expressions in each pair are equivalent.

1. xy and yx **2.** $3(a + b)$ and $3a + b$

3. $2x - y$ and $y - 2x$

4. $5(a - b)$ and $5a - 5b$

5. $x - 2y$ and $-2y + x$

6. $6(a + b) + a$ and $7a + 6b$

7. $2x + 3y$ and $5x$

8. $\dfrac{x}{y}$ and $\dfrac{y}{x}$ **9.** $\dfrac{1}{3}x$ and $\dfrac{1}{3x}$

10. Which expressions are equivalent to the expression $2(x - y)$?

  a. $2y - 2x$ **b.** $2x - 2y$

  c. $2x - y$ **d.** $x + x - 2y$

11. Which expressions are equivalent to the expression $2a + 5(b - a)$?

  a. $2a + 5(a - b)$ **b.** $5b - 3a$

  c. $a + 5b$ **d.** $-3a + 5b$

12. Which expressions are equivalent to the expression $3x + 2y - x$?

  a. $2x + 2y$ **b.** $2y + 2x$

  c. $2(x + y)$ **d.** $4x$

Extending Concepts

13. The seats in a certain type of airplane are arranged as shown. The number of rows, r, and the width of the middle section, a, vary from plane to plane.

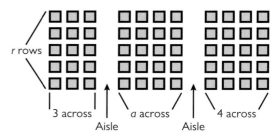

a. Write an equation for the total number of seats, s, on an airplane. Your equation should tell how s is related to r and a.

b. Write at least two different equations equivalent to your equation in part **a**.

c. Check that your equations are equivalent by substituting values for a and r. Show your work. Use at least three different pairs for a and r.

Writing

14. Answer the letter to Dr. Math.

> Dear Dr. Math:
>
> I wanted to test the equivalence of the expressions $x(y - 1)$ and $xy - 1$.
> I decided to substitute values for x and y. I picked $x = 1$, $y = 2$. For both expressions, the result was 1. Then I picked $x = 1$, $y = 5$. For both expressions, the result was 4. So then I figured that the expressions must be equivalent. Am I right?
> P. Luggin

The Top-Selling Albums of All Time, Part 1

Applying Skills

1. In 1996, an album's total sales are 20 million, and its current rate of sale is 0.1 million per year.

   a. Make a table showing total sales 0, 1, 2, 3, 4, and 10 years after 1996.

   b. Describe how you can find the total sales for any given number of years after 1996.

   c. Write an equation that relates x, the number of years after 1996, to y, the total sales (in millions) for that year.

   d. Use your equation to predict the album's total sales in the year 2035.

2. In 1996, an album's total sales are 15 million, and its current rate of sale is 50,000 per week. If the album sells 50,000 copies in one week, how many are sold in one year? How can you write this amount as a number of millions?

3. Repeat items **1a–d** for the album described in item **2**.

Extending Concepts

4. On January 1, 1996, the population of a country is 22.8 million and increasing at 2,500 per week.

   a. By how much does the population increase in a year?

   b. By how many millions does the population increase in a year?

   c. Make a table showing the population (in millions) 0, 1, 2, 3, 4, and 5 years after January 1, 1996. Give each population to the nearest hundredth.

   d. Write an equation that relates x, the number of years after January 1, 1996, to y, the population (in millions).

   e. Use your equation to predict the population on January 1, 2026, and on July 1, 2026.

   f. What assumptions are you making in part **e**? Do you think these are reasonable? Why or why not?

Writing

5. Write a summary of what you have learned in this phase about expressions, equations, variables, and inequalities. Be sure to explain the difference between an expression and an equation and the difference between an equation and an inequality. Also, describe how you can tell whether two expressions are equivalent.

Seeing Things Graphically

Applying Skills

1. For each point shown on the coordinate plane, give its coordinates and tell which quadrant it lies in.

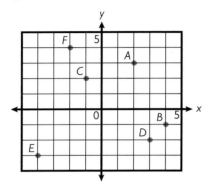

2. Plot each point on a coordinate plane.

   a. $(3, 4)$ **b.** $(2, -1)$ **c.** $(-3, 1)$

   d. $(-2, -4)$ **e.** $(3, 0)$ **f.** $(0, -1)$

Tell whether each statement is true or false. Explain your thinking.

3. The x-coordinate of the point $(-1, 3)$ is -1.

4. The point $(-1, 4)$ lies in the fourth quadrant.

5. The point $(-3, -8)$ lies in the third quadrant.

6. Any point whose y-coordinate is positive lies above the x-axis.

7. Any point whose x-coordinate is negative lies below the x-axis.

8. Any point that has a y-coordinate of 0 lies on the y-axis.

9. Any point whose x-coordinate is positive lies in the first quadrant.

Extending Concepts

10. a. Make a table of values that satisfy the equation $y = x + 3$.

   b. Write the pairs of numbers from your table as ordered pairs.

   c. Plot the points on a coordinate grid. Does it make sense to draw a line through the points?

   d. Do you think that if you extended your line, the point $(100, 103)$ would lie on the line? Why or why not?

   e. If a point lies on the line, what can you say about its coordinates?

Writing

11. Answer the letter to Dr. Math.

> Dear Dr. Math,
>
> My teacher asked for the coordinates of two points that lie on the x-axis. I figured that all points on the x-axis must have an x-coordinate of 0. So I wrote (0, 4) and (0, 98). My friend, Lou, said that I got it wrong. He said that points on the x-axis actually have a y-coordinate of 0. That sounds pretty silly to me. If Lou is right, why would they call it the x-axis? Who is right?
>
> Muriel

The Algebra Walk

Applying Skills

Suppose that in the Algebra Walk, the walkers calculate their walking number according to one of the instructions below.

A. Multiply starting number by 2 and add 1.

B. Multiply starting number by -2.

C. Multiply starting number by -2 and subtract 1.

D. Multiply starting number by 3.

Which set or sets of instructions are possible if . . .

1. the person with starting number 3 walks forward 7 units?

2. the person standing at the origin does not move?

3. after the Algebra Walk, nobody is standing at the origin?

4. the walkers with positive starting numbers walk backwards?

5. the students end up in a line that slopes downwards from left to right?

6. the student with starting number 2 walks 3 units farther than the student with starting number 1?

For each of the equations below, make a table of values that fit the equation. Then make a graph of the equation.

7. $y = 3x$

8. $y = -3x$

9. $y = 3x + 2$

10. $y = 3x - 2$

11. $y = 2x + 3$

12. $y = -2x + 3$

Extending Concepts

13. Write three equations whose graphs are lines that do not go through the origin. What do the equations have in common? Why does this make sense?

14. Write three equations whose graphs are lines that slant downwards from left to right. What do the equations have in common?

15. Write three equations whose graphs are lines that are steeper than the graph of $y = 5x$. What do the equations have in common?

Making Connections

16. When sound travels in air, its speed is about 12.4 miles per minute. Suppose that sound travels for x minutes. Let y represent the distance (in miles) that it travels. Then x and y are related by the equation $y = 12.4x$. Make a table of values that fit this equation and make a graph of the equation.

Putting It All Together

Applying Skills

Tell whether the graph of each equation is a horizontal line, a vertical line, or neither.

1. $y = 2x$ **2.** $x = 4$

3. $y = -5$ **4.** $y = -3x + 2$

5. $y = 7$ **6.** $x = 0$

Translate each equation into words. Then make a table of values and a graph.

7. $y = 3$ **8.** $x = -1$

9. $y = -4$ **10.** $y = 2x$

11. $y = 0$ **12.** $x = 5$

13. $y = -3x + 2$ **14.** $x = 0$

For each line in items **15** and **16** do the following: (a) Find the coordinates of five points on the line; (b) Make a table of x and y values from these coordinates; (c) Write the equation of the line.

15.

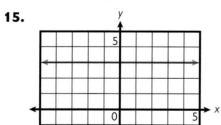

16.

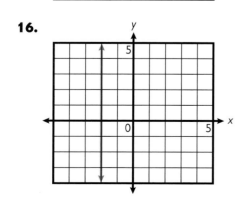

Extending Concepts

17. a. In addition to the equation on page 21, the relationship between Fahrenheit and Celsius can also be described by the equation $C = \frac{5}{9}(F - 32)$. Describe this relationship in words.

   b. Make a table showing at least five pairs of values for Fahrenheit (F) and Celsius (C).

   c. Make a graph of the equation. Show Fahrenheit temperature on the horizontal axis. Choose the scale on the horizontal axis so that Fahrenheit temperatures ranging from 0° to 100° are included.

   d. Pick a new point on the graph (one that is not included in your table in part **b**) and estimate its coordinates. Check the coordinates by using the equation. Explain how you did this.

Writing

18. Write a summary of what you have learned about coordinates, equations, tables, and graphs. Include an explanation of how you can graph the equation of a line. Also, describe how you can tell when the graph of an equation will be a horizontal or vertical line.

The Top-Selling Albums of All Time, Part 2

Applying Skills

Suppose that in 1996 an album's total sales are 2.5 million and that the album is currently selling 0.125 million copies per month.

1. How many copies is the album selling per year?

2. Make a table that shows the total sales for the album 0, 1, 2, 3, 4, and 5 years after 1996.

3. Write an equation relating x, the number of years after 1996, and y, the album's total sales (in millions).

4. Draw axes and choose a scale for the x-axis and y-axis. The x-axis should show the number of years after 1996, and the y-axis should show the total sales.

5. Plot points from your table in item 2 to help make a graph of the album's sales.

6. Use your graph to estimate the album's total sales in the year 2005.

Extending Concepts

7. How would your graph in item 5 be different if the album was currently selling 0.2 million copies per month instead of 0.125 million?

8. Do you think that your estimate in item 6 is likely to be too low or too high? Why?

Making Connections

In 1995, the world population was approximately 5.7 billion and was increasing by about 0.09 billion people per year.

9. Make a table showing the world population (in billions) 0, 1, 2, 3, 4, and 5 years after 1995.

10. Make a graph of the world population. The x-axis should show the number of years beyond 1995, and the y-axis should show the world population. The graph should extend at least to the year 2005.

11. Use your graph to predict the world population in 2005.

12. Do you think that the world population would really follow a straight line, or do you think that one of the graphs shown here might be more realistic? Explain your thinking.

a.
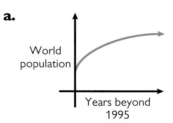

b.
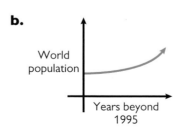

Situations and Solutions

Applying Skills

At his summer job, Rashad is paid a one-time bonus of $15 plus $8 per hour.

1. Make a table of values showing the number of hours Rashad works (*h*) and the corresponding total salary he receives (*s*).

2. Write an equation that describes the relationship between *s* and *h*.

3. Make a graph that shows the relationship between *s* and *h*.

4. How many hours would Rashad have to work to earn each amount?

a. $63	**b.** $31	**c.** $67
d. $35	**e.** $87	**f.** $47

Working at her father's office, Tonya is paid a one-time bonus of $20 plus $9.50 per hour.

5. Repeat items **1–3** for Tonya's job.

6. How many hours would Tonya have to work to earn each amount?

a. $58	**b.** $67.50	**c.** $43.75
d. $48.50	**e.** $77	**f.** $81.75

Extending Concepts

7. a. Describe a general rule you can use to figure out the number of hours Rashad must work to make any given amount of money.

b. Describe how you can use your graph in item **3** to figure out the number of hours Rashad must work to make any given amount of money.

c. Suppose you want to know how many hours Rashad must work to make $44.60. Can you find an exact solution using your rule from part **a**? Using your graph? Why or why not?

8. a. Use your graph to figure out how many hours Tonya must work to make $86.50. Explain your method.

b. Check your solution to part **a** by using your equation. Show your work.

Writing

9. Answer the letter to Dr. Math.

> Dear Dr. Math,
> An advertisement said I could rent a video camera for a fee of $12 plus $5 per hour. I have $42 and am trying to figure out how long I can rent that camera. Can you help?
> Future Movie Director

Solving Simple Equations and Inequalities

homework 10

Applying Skills

Find the value of x that solves each equation. Check your solution by substituting it back into the equation.

1. $4x + 3 = 11$ **2.** $4 + 2x = 10$

3. $3x + 5 = 26$ **4.** $-1 + 2x = 19$

5. $1.5x + 3 = 18$ **6.** $-5 + 7x = 30$

7. $4x + 7 = 35$ **8.** $-6x = 18$

9. $-2x + 3 = 7$ **10.** $5x + 8 = 38$

11. $2 + 3x = -10$ **12.** $-3x + 6 = 15$

Find the values of x that make each inequality true. Graph each solution on a number line.

13. $3x < 9$ **14.** $x + 2 < 5$

15. $x - 3 \geq 1$ **16.** $4x > 8$

17. $x - 2 > 0$ **18.** $2x + 4 \leq 8$

19. $x + 3 \leq 1$ **20.** $2x \geq 6$

21. $3x - 1 \geq 2$

Extending Concepts

Write each equation or inequality using symbols. Then solve the equation or inequality and explain how you solved it.

22. Ten more than x is 23.

23. Six times y plus 2 is 20.

24. Twice m is less than 6.

25. Two less than x is greater than 7.

Writing

26. Answer the letter to Dr. Math.

> Dear Dr. Math,
>
> My friend, Lee, and I were trying to solve the equation $4x + 2 = 21$. Lee began by saying, "Something plus 2 equals 21, so that 'something' must be equal to 19." Then he wrote $4x = 19$ and said, "4 times something is 19." I told him to stop right there— no number multiplied by 4 will give you 19. So, I think he made a mistake somewhere. Can you help us?
>
> E. Quation

The Balancing Act

Applying Skills

Each picture shows a balanced scale. In each picture, all cups contain the same (unknown) number of marbles. Figure out how many marbles a cup contains.

1.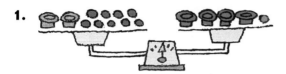

2.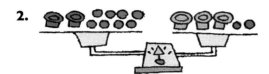

3.

4.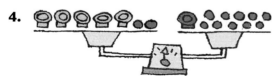

Solve each equation using any method. Keep a step-by-step record of your work and check your solution.

5. $3x + 8 = 4x + 1$

6. $2y + 8 = 5y + 2$

7. $3r + 13 = 7r + 1$

8. $5t + 7 = t + 9$

9. $x + 9 = 3x - 1$

10. $3x + 2 = 4x - 4$

Draw a balance picture for each equation and solve the equation.

11. $3m + 9 = 5m + 3$

12. $4x + 3 = 2x + 4$

13. $5y + 1 = 4y + 10$

Extending Concepts

Bernie's Bicycles rents bicycles for $10 plus $4 per hour.

14. You have $26. Write an equation that will give you the number of hours that you could rent a bike.

15. Draw a balance picture for the equation and then solve the equation.

Writing

16. Answer the letter to Dr. Math.

> Dear Dr. Math,
>
> I solved the inequality $2x \geq 3$ by testing lots of different values for x. I found that if x is 2, 3, 4, 5 or any larger number, the inequality is true. If x is 1, 0, or a negative number, it is false. So I figured that the solution to the inequality must be $x \geq 2$. Was this a good way to solve the inequality? What do you think?
>
> Jean Luc

The Top-Selling Albums of All Time, Part 3

Applying Skills

Suppose that in 1996 an album's total sales are 4 million and that the album is currently selling 0.02 million copies per month. You want to know when total sales will reach 25 million.

1. How many copies is the album currently selling per year?

2. Make a table that shows the future sales of the album. Do not include every year, but be sure to include the year in which sales hit (or pass) 25 million copies.

3. Make a graph of the future sales of the album. Your graph should show when sales hit 25 million.

4. Use your table and graph to predict when total sales will hit 25 million.

5. Write an equation that describes the future sales of the album.

6. Modify the equation so that it tells when sales will be 25 million.

7. Solve the equation. Show the steps you used to find the solution.

8. Based on your answer to item **7**, predict when sales will hit 25 million. How accurate do you think your prediction is?

Extending Concepts

The graph shows the total sales of an album.

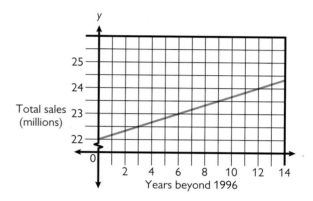

9. Approximately how many albums will be sold by the year 2002?

10. In what year will the sales of the album reach 24 million copies?

Writing

11. Answer the letter to Dr. Math.

> Dear Dr. Math,
> When I solved the equation $2x + 1 = 17$, I drew a balance picture and wound up finding that $x = 8$. I checked my solution, so I know it's right, but someone told me I could have solved the equation a different way. What other ways could I have done it?
> Sally D. Solver

STUDENT
GALLERY

CREDITS: Photography: Chris Conroy • Beverley Harper (cover).
Illustrations: Argus Childers, pp. 2, 19, 23, 26, 27, 30–32, 44.

Creative Publications and MathScape are trademarks or registered trademarks of Creative Publications.

© 1998 Creative Publications

Two Prudential Plaza, Suite 1175
Chicago, IL 60601

Printed in the United States of America.

ISBN: 0-7622-0225-4

4 5 6 7 8 9 10.02 01 00